LEARNING THROUGH PLAY

Circle time

HANNAH MORTIMER

Published by Scholastic Ltd,
Villiers House,
Clarendon Avenue,
Leamington Spa,
Warwickshire CV32 5PR
Text © Hannah Mortimer
© 1998 Scholastic Ltd
3 4 5 6 7 8 9 0   9 0 1 2 3 4 5 6 7

Author
Hannah Mortimer

Editor
Jane Bishop

Assistant Editor
Clare Miller

Series designer
Lynne Joesbury

Designer
Mark Udall

Illustrations
Sami Sweeten

Cover photograph
© Digital Vision

Designed using Adobe Pagemaker

British Library Cataloguing-in-Publication Data
A catalogue record for this book is available from the British Library.

ISBN 0-590-53914-0

CONTENTS

CHAPTER FIVE: PHYSICAL DEVELOPMENT

CHAPTER SIX: CREATIVE DEVELOPMENT

PHOTOCOPIABLES

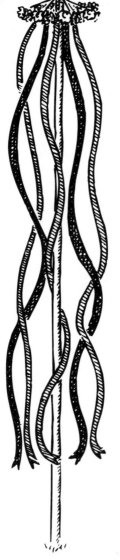

Why 'circle time'?

'Circle time' is an ideal opportunity to bring many members of the group together to share their play and learning with each other. Within the circle, children learn to look and to listen, to learn from each other and to develop an identity with the rest of the group. The use of 'circle time' activities in developing children's self-esteem and confidence is now well established. In this book, those same approaches are used to develop children's understanding across every area of learning. 'Circle time' is an excellent means of developing social skills and co-operation, regardless of which area of the curriculum is being covered.

Learning through play

This book has been designed to meet the *Desirable Outcomes for Children's Learning*, as recommended by SCAA and used in England. However, the ideas in this book can be applied equally well to the guidance documents on pre-school education published for Wales, Scotland and Northern Ireland. *Circle time* will provide practical ideas for activities which children and adults can enjoy within a circle across all learning areas, from Language and Literacy through to Creative Development. For example:

Language and Literacy – develop language skills during circle time by encouraging attentive listening, providing opportunities to respond to rhyme and story and giving the children the chance to share their personal experiences. Children can begin to associate sounds with patterns in rhymes and to develop confidence in expressing themselves through word games and discussion.

Mathematics – practise early counting skills in a fun and non-threatening way within the circle. Games involving position and space can help to develop early mathematical language, and there will be opportunities for exploring number rhymes, songs and stories.

Personal and Social Development – circles provide an ideal setting to encourage sharing and turn-taking. Children learn to feel comfortable within the routines of 'circle time' and to know what is expected of them. They are able to help and support each other through their ideas and actions, and to share a range of responses and feelings arising from the activities.

Knowledge and Understanding of the World – use 'circle time' as an opportunity to introduce talk on many topics of interest. Children can talk about their worlds, their families and their communities. They can explore their worlds through songs and rhymes and explore features of living things through animal games.

Physical Development – within the circle, children can learn to move confidently and with imagination. Action rhymes and rhythm games provide opportunities for practising many fine and large movements, and teach the skills of watching and copying others. Small toys and musical instruments can be handled and passed, each child inspiring the confidence of the next.

Creative Development – provide opportunities for hatching and sharing good ideas in the circle. Children can explore sounds and movements, and respond in a variety of ways to what they see, hear, smell, touch and feel. The circle will also enable you to develop opportunities for using music and dance.

Setting up the environment

You will need a comfortable floor space, free from obstacles or too many distractions, for your 'circle time' activities. Provide a carpeted area to sit on, preferably with screens or tables separating the space from the rest of the play area. Consider using a quiet book or story area which can double up well. At first, young children find it difficult to sit in a circle, especially if there are many of them. Try positioning small cushions or carpet square samples to mark their places. Where there is enough space, you can also use small chairs placed in a circle, but take care that the adults do not tower above the children.

Make sure you have anything you need for the activity behind you so that you do not have to break the circle by stepping over the children to fetch it. You could keep a treasure chest handy so that your props remain a surprise until you are ready to use them. If you have some very young or unsure children, let them sit on a knee and observe the circle for a session or two, gradually involving them as they become more confident. If you have very active children, consider running two smaller 'circle time' groups, keeping the activities short and engaging. Aim to bring the whole group together once all the children are ready.

Always time the 'circle time' activity to end on a successful note before the children become fidgety; ten minutes at the very most.

Using adult helpers

'Circle time' is best used by everyone sharing an activity together, so include adult helpers in the circle, preferably sitting on the floor with the children. If you have visitors that day, consider inviting them to join you too. Arrange the helpers so that they are sitting beside the younger children or any children who need support for special needs. Whilst you are busy presenting the materials and leading the discussion, the adult helpers can focus the children's attention, using encouragement to hold their interest and

praising their involvement. If it is essential that other adults are busy in another part of the room, ask them to move quietly and unobtrusively so that the children's concentration is not interrupted.

Young children may find it difficult to pass things around a circle as they will be unsure in which direction the items should go. If the activity involves passing round a toy or object, then use a 'circle time' teddy or mascot to give the children a demonstration. Ask your helpers to show the children how to pass a teddy round in a given direction, and send round Teddy as a reminder before the object is passed. The teddy can also be used to help turn-taking when speaking if this is a problem for your group; whoever holds the teddy now is the speaker, and the others should listen.

Observation and assessment

The Desirable Outcomes are designed to tell us what we should expect children to be able to do by the term after their fifth birthdays. Ideas in this book provide 'circle time' activities designed to fulfil the learning outcomes expected by SCAA. The circle gives you an ideal opportunity to observe all the children at once and see what they can or cannot do. This provides information on what skills individual children are lacking and with which they need further support. If you personally are leading the group, ask one of your adult helpers to observe the children in order to gather information on individual children's progress for their Record of Achievement. Take photographs to provide useful evidence of how the children responded and joined in, and also as a useful way of explaining 'circle time' to your parents and visitors.

Links with home

Many of the activities in this book contain suggestions for linking the activity to home or involving the children's families. Sometimes children are invited to bring in a special possession, to talk with their parents about a topic of interest, or to take ideas home to share. Use a regular newsletter to keep your parents in touch with what you have been doing and ways in which they can help their children with future activities. When children share favourite toys or memories from home within the circle, they are helped to feel valued and confident within the group.

Mount some of your 'circle time' photographs to provide a display to explain why you use this approach and how it helps all the children with their social skills and co-operation. Do find opportunities to involve parent helpers and visitors in the circle itself; this can be a useful way of helping the children relate to a wider range of adults in a familiar situation. Pass round your 'circle time' teddy at the start of the activity so that each child and visitor can tell Teddy their name. You can round off your activities by saying 'goodbye' to Teddy as well. This adds a structure to the 'circle time' and makes sure every child, adult and parent is actively included in it.

Meeting special needs

'Circle time' activities are ideal for helping children with special needs to look, listen, and to feel a valued member of a group. They provide a useful way of including all children in activities regardless of their special needs or previous experiences. Make sure that any child with particular needs has an adult helper close by if needed, and ensure that the helper knows what you are aiming the child to achieve from the activity. This might be a particular teaching target from the child's Individual Education Plan, or it might be a more general goal such as helping the child to feel confident in a large group, or encouraging attention. The adult should help to direct the child's attention, and use praise and encouragement to let the child feel successful.

All of the activities carry suggestions for adapting the activity for younger children. Many of these ideas will be helpful for including children with special needs, but remember always to keep the activity age-appropriate for the child whose development might be delayed.

Health and safety

Always make sure the children wear the right clothes and footwear for the activity. In some of the more physical activities, you will see suggestions that the children should wear suitable PE clothing or plimsolls. In this way, you can ensure that

children do not move too fast for their own safety on slippery surfaces. You will need to warn parents ahead if special clothing is needed.

Keep the floor areas where you meet for 'circle time' clean and clear from obstacles. Give clear rules to make sure that children do not tread on each other's fingers or toes if they are required to move from or in your circle. Encourage them to join and then drop hands in a circle to help to introduce the idea of staying a little way apart from each other. Keep a watchful eye out for any children who need your special attention and support; 'circle time' is an excellent way to build up children's confidence, but some will need your constant encouragement to make sure this happens.

When you are passing small objects around the circle, make sure that they are safe, that there are no loose parts or sharp edges which could harm the children. Place any objects outside the circle once you have finished talking about them before starting your next activity. If you are smelling fragrances, make sure they are not harmful to the children, bearing in mind any possible allergies or medical difficulties.

How to use this book

The activities which you will find in this book have all been written to help you work towards the Desirable Outcomes for children's learning. The six chapters coincide with the six areas of learning, and there are eight activities in each chapter. The topic web on page 10 shows which activities relate to each area of learning. However, there are many occasions when there is overlap between areas so that any one activity can relate to many areas of learning at once. This integrated approach is particularly helpful for children's learning.

Dip into the activities to suit a particular topic or theme you are following. You can use the ideas flexibly, adding your own details and personal touches, and adapting them to suit your children and your situation. The most exciting and impressionable 'circle times' are those where the children themselves develop ideas and take you with them. Try to look for learning opportunities and allow the activity to take off on a tangent if the children are learning usefully and the situation is well under control.

PERSONAL AND SOCIAL DEVELOPMENT

LANGUAGE & LITERACY

PHYSICAL DEVELOPMENT

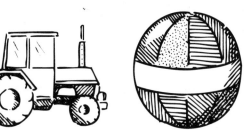

MATHEMATICS

CIRCLE TIME

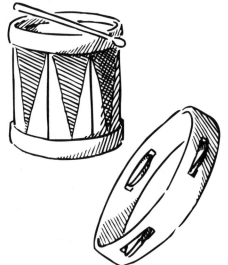

KNOWLEDGE AND UNDERSTANDING OF THE WORLD

CREATIVE DEVELOPMENT

Encourage listening and responding, developing vocabulary skills and awareness of the rhythm and rhyme of language with these activities. 'Circle time' is used here to help children to listen more attentively and talk more confidently.

WHO'S LISTENING NOW?

Learning Objective
To develop skills of listening and responding.

Group size
The whole group.

What you need
Your attendance register and a pen.

Setting up
Gather the children in a circle at a regular time each session. Mark spaces with cushions or carpet sample squares if the children find this difficult.

What to do
Take your attendance register in a way which encourages full attention and listening from the children. Open your register, but do not call the children's names in a regular order. Instead, call the names in any order using two notes to make a cuck–oo' sound: 'Jas-on', 'Jamil–a'. Help the children echo your notes with a reply 'Hel-lo' and look up to greet each child with a look and a smile. Make a note in your register as each child answers. Every now and then, call a child's name for a second time and encourage the echo. This keeps everyone looking and listening until registration is over.

Questions to ask
Pause every now and then to make a personal comment to each child: Are you better now? Was that your little sister with Mum? Your hair looks smart; have you had it cut? Didn't you work hard at your model yesterday!

For younger children
Echo the 'hel-lo' with them until they are ready to answer themselves. Do not insist on a solo performance!

For older children
Let older children try to call out each other's names themselves. Finish by adding any names which have been left out.

Follow-up activities
● Play a game where you call a child's name and roll a ball across the circle to that child, to help the children listen out for their own names (page 44).
● Pass Teddy round the circle so that each child can tell him their names and say 'hello'.
● Have a whispering version of register so that the children have to listen especially carefully.

GOOD NEWS

Learning objective
To talk about familiar experiences.

Group size
Start with six children: increase to include the whole group.

What you need
Ask parents to encourage their children to bring a 'show-and-tell' item. This could be anything which is important to them such as a holiday photograph, a present, a seed they have grown, an interesting treasure they have found.

Setting up
Provide the children with somewhere safe to keep anything brought from home until it is time to share their news.

What to do
Start with a small group of six children and work up to a larger group involving all the children as their confidence grows.

Warn the children that 'circle time' is about to begin and ask them to bring their 'show and tell' things to the circle, placing them carefully behind them as they sit in the circle. Go round the circle inviting children who have brought something in to show it and talk about it. Invite them to sit next to you as they do so, so that you can help and encourage them. Pass the item round the circle if the child has given permission, for the other children to admire.

Questions to ask
Ask the child to tell you all about their item. Why did they choose to bring it in? What made it special? Ask the other children to share their experiences, and encourage them to ask questions.

For younger children
If a child is shy or has difficulties in expressing themselves, have a private word with parents. Ask them to send something in for the child to share but also tell you about it. You will then be able to help the child by asking simple 'yes'/'no' questions or, as confidence develops, questions which offer a choice: 'Was it fun on the roundabout or a bit scary?'

For older children
Ask questions which are open-ended and require more than a 'yes' or 'no' reply: 'Tell us what was happening in this photograph' or 'Tell us why you liked this present so much'.

Follow-up activities
● Help the children start a photograph album or illustrated news book and write in the captions as they dictate them.
● Have a pigeon hole or section of shelf where each child can leave any treasures from home. Label the shelf, and encourage the children to respect each other's private space.
● Use 'circle time' to encourage the children to share news about what has happened in the group, as well as sharing good news about home.

THE TOY SHOP GAME

Learning objective
To develop vocabulary
and memory.

Group size
Up to four children.

What you need
A selection of twelve small toys, these might include: a train, a car, a teddy, a box of crayons, a rattle, a ball, some bubbles in a pot, a cartoon figure, a picture book, a pot of modelling dough, a doll, a tractor. A shopping bag which you cannot see through and a tray.

Setting up
Arrange the toys on a tray so that they can all be seen easily. Gather the children in a circle on the floor.

What to do
Tell the children you are going to play a game about a toy shop. Invite each child to choose an item from the tray which they might buy in a toy shop. Ask them to hold on to it, and then place the tray with the remaining toys behind you and out of the circle.

Pass the shopping bag round and help each child say, 'I went to the toy shop and I bought...' Then help them say the word for their toy and place it inside the bag. The next child should say their toy and also the name of the toy which the previous child has placed in the bag. If they cannot remember, allow them a quick peak into the bag to remind them. Continue around the circle, building the list up by one toy each time. Stop when the bag comes back to you. Repeat the game four times with a new selection of toys and starting with a new child each time.

Questions to ask
Can you remember what Hanif put in? What did we call Samantha's toy? Talk about remembering, and see how many things the children can remember from when they were very young. How do grown-ups remember what to buy when they go shopping?

For younger children
Repeat the game with the same four toys rather than extending the choice to twelve.

For older children
Introduce items which have unusual names to remember, such as a stethoscope, a kaleidoscope and a tambourine. Repeat the game without props so that the children have to remember the items without being prompted.

Follow-up activities
● Provide paper and crayons and play at list-making. Encourage the children to find different ways of making lists: mark-making, cut-out pictures, cut-out sections of packaging, drawings.
● Ask the children to remember three things to bring in from home.
● Give the children messages for them to try to remember from one 'circle time' to another.

RHYME TIME

Learning objective
*To listen to rhyming
words.*

Group size
Six to 18 children.

What you need
A selection of toys or objects: a cat, a train, a ball, a dog, a box, a car, a tin and a cup (you can select more once you are familiar with the activity).

Setting up
Arrange the items in the centre of the circle, encouraging the children to look but not touch.

What to do
Ask the children if they have ever played the game 'I-spy' before. Tell them that this activity is similar but it is all about sounds which rhyme. Explain that sounds which rhyme are sounds which sound the same and give them some examples: cat and hat, dog and log, cup and pup. Then introduce the game by repeating this phrase:

I spy, with my little eye,
something which sounds like......

Choose a word which rhymes with one of your items.

Use your eyes to indicate the relevant item as you pause for the children to speak the answer. They will find this very hard at first, so help them by repeating pairs of words and encouraging them to listen; 'hat, dog.....do they sound the same?' Celebrate their eventual success and repeat the activity for all the other items.

Questions to ask
Ask the children to think of other words which rhyme with each item. Can they think of any rhymes for their own names? Can they think of a part of their body which rhymes with 'toes' (prompt this with the initial letter sound /n/).

For younger children
Keep the group small (four to six children). Choose a pair of items which sound very different, such as 'cat' and 'shoe'. Gradually increase the choice and select items with similar sounds as the children become more used to the activity. For very young children, you might have to begin by teaching the word 'same'; do this by having two of each object and inviting the children to find you 'another the same as this one' until they understand.

For older children
Older children will enjoy having a turn at leading this activity, finding their own examples of rhyming sounds.

Follow-up activities
● Cut out or draw pictures, including a hat, bat, mat, and rat. Mount these on a large sheet of paper and challenge the children to point to all the sounds which rhyme with 'cat'.
● Look for the rhyming words in well-known songs and nursery rhymes.
● Collect toys and objects with similar sounds: cat, hat, mat, dog, frog, log and so on. Put hoops on the floor and ask the children to collect together those items which rhyme into separate hoops.

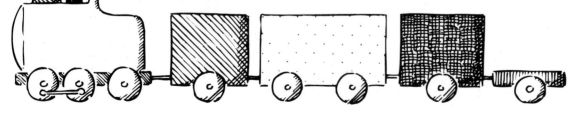

MY FAVOURITE BOOK

Learning objective
To share a favourite book with the other children.

Group size
Six to eight children.

What you need
Ask the children to take turns in bringing one of their favourite books to 'circle time'.

Setting up
In your newsletter tell parents that you will be inviting children to bring in a favourite book from home to share with the group, then ask one parent and child to arrange this each session. If it is easier, or if the child prefers, let the children choose a book from your book corner. Encourage parents to talk with their child about the book so that their child can tell everyone else why they enjoyed the story and pictures so much.

What to do
Invite the child who has brought along their book to sit next to you in the circle. Admire the book and read it to all the children, sharing the pictures. Talk about the book afterwards and thank the child for choosing it.

Questions to ask
Why did you choose this book? What do you like best about it? Ask the other children if they enjoyed it too, and see if they can remember it. Who is it about? What happens in the story? What do you think will happen next?

For younger children
Use the pictures to prompt your questions. Who is this? What is happening in this picture?

For older children
Invite them to turn the pages for the other children to see and use their own words to tell the story.

Follow-up activities
● Have a theme day where you all dress up as your favourite characters from a book.
● Invite the children to make a picture or collage to illustrate their favourite book and write the title in for them.
● Keep your pictures in a special scrap book which the children can look at to remember all the favourite books they have talked about.

MAGIC WANDS

Learning objective
To develop confidence in role play.

Group size
Six to 12 children.

What you need
A sparkly 'magic' wand.

Setting up
Gather the children standing in a circle for this activity.

What to do
Tell the children that you are going to play a game. Start by showing the children what you mean: tell them that you are about to wave a 'magic' wand and you would like them all to pretend to be babies. Explain that when you clap your hands, they should stop pretending and be themselves again. Have a practice, changing them into babies and then cats!

Now invite each child to think of something they would really like to be: a singer, a puppy dog, a teacher, a policeman, a dancer or a tiger. Wave your 'magic' wand and change all the children into that person/animal, allowing them to move within the circle space; returning to their places when you clap your hands. Allow each child to take a turn in choosing what they should all become.

Questions to ask
Ask the children what it felt like when they were pretending to be someone else. Did you feel very wild when you were a tiger? What did you do when you were a teacher? Were you a mischievous puppy?

For younger children
Keep the ideas very simple, perhaps pretending to be different animals on 'Old Macdonald's Farm'.

For older children
Make the ideas more complex and develop a place for the pretend play. Where would the children really like to be? Help the children act out a whole situation, perhaps arriving at a birthday party, or playing on the beach.

Follow-up activities
● Help the children act out a favourite story, building in their own ideas and perhaps videoing it for the parents to see.
● Help the children think of their own actions and sound effects for a favourite rhyme or song.
● Provide an imaginary play space in which you change the props regularly; a home corner can change to a shop, to a hairdresser's, to an office, to a hospital, or to a classroom.

TRAIN GAME

Learning objective
To learn to copy the rhythm of words and phrases.

Group size
Eight to 15 children.

What you need
A comfortable floor mat so that you can all sit in a circle.

What to do
Tell the children that you have made up a funny rhyme that includes a lot of your favourite foods. Explain that the way you say the rhyme sounds like a train speeding up!

Ask the children to sit in a circle with you and any adult helpers. Invite the children to start by moving their arms like the pistons of a heavy steam train, repeating everything you say. Start the rhythm of this chant slowly, and gradually build up speed and momentum until the final 'soup' sounds like the whistle of the train.

Coffee, coffee, coffee, coffee,
Cheese and biscuits, cheese and biscuits, cheese and biscuits, cheese and biscuits,
Chocolate pudding, chocolate pudding, chocolate pudding, chocolate pudding,
Bangers and mash! bangers and mash! bangers and mash! bangers and mash!
SOOOOOUP!

Questions to ask
Who has travelled on a train? Did you enjoy it? What other things could we think of for our train game? Shall we see if the words make a good train sound if we say them the same way? Do you think this would make a good dinner to eat? Do you have a pudding before your sausages?!

For younger children
Encourage them to focus on making the piston movements and join in with the 'SOOOUP!'

For older children
Give them time to think about alternative words and then let them teach their version to the other children and adults.

Follow-up activities
● Make a train with a line of chairs; encourage the children to pretend getting on the train, taking their luggage with them.
● Test some percussion instruments and find the best sounds to accompany the rhythm of the chant.

HUSH! HUSH!

Learning objective
To encourage attentive listening within a large group.

Group size
12 to 15 children.

What you need
The photocopiable story sheet on page 59.

Setting up
Make a copy of the sheet for each child, and use one yourself to tell the story.

What to do
Tell the children you are going to tell them a story, but a lot of the words are missing. Can the children help to guess what the words are? Explain that whenever they see you put your finger to your lips and hear you say 'sssh!', they should think very carefully what word might be missing. Tell them to keep it a secret and not shout out.

Read each sentence, making a 'sssh!' sound wherever you see a picture. Encourage the children to think what the missing word is but not to tell you yet. Then tell them you will read the words once more and the children can fill in the gaps. Read the sentence once more and say the missing word along with the chorus of voices.

Repeat for each sentence. This activity is a simple version of the 'cloze' method which helps in development of reading skills.

Questions to ask
Can the children think of any other words which might fit? Was it easy guessing the word? What helped them guess?

For younger children
Gather the younger children together in one group, and give each of them a copy of the activity sheet so that they can all see a picture clue each time.

For older children
Instead of doing the activity sentence by sentence, tell the whole story with gaps and then repeat it so that the children can join in with the missing words as you read.

Follow-up activities
● Pause occasionally when you are telling a story and ask the children to guess the missing word; talk about how they decided which word to suggest.
● In familiar stories with repeated words and phrases, pause in places for the children to join in with you.
● Give the children the story sheet to take home and 'read' with their parents. Ask parents to point to the written words as they read them, pausing for their child to volunteer the word which will replace the picture.

MATHEMATICS

Use 'circle time' to teach early number skills with ideas to encourage children to count and to recognize numerals. Try some games for sorting, matching and sequencing, and introduce some useful vocabulary relating to position and space.

THREE GREEN JELLYFISH

Learning objective
To practise counting to three using fingers to help.

Group size
Up to ten children.

What you need
A tambourine.

What to do
This activity is an excellent and enjoyable way to grasp the children's attention at the beginning of 'circle time'.

Ask the children to sit down and wobble like a jelly. Tell them to shake all over when your tambourine shakes and stop when you beat it. Try this two or three times until the children are fully relaxed and attentive. Praise them as they look and listen.

Now tell them you are going to sing a song about three jellyfish. Ask them to count to three with you. Help them to hold out all their fingers of one hand, and to use their index finger on their other hand to count out with you 'one, two, three' as they point to each finger, starting at the thumb. Ask a helper to move behind them and prompt. The children are now ready to say the rhyme. Encourage them to shake like a jelly each time they say the word 'jellyfish'.

Three green jellyfish, three green jellyfish, (all together)
Three green jellyfish, lying on the beach. (all together)
Then one of them decided to go for a swim, and he went... (spoken by you)
Wibble wobble wibble wobble SPLOSH! Down into the sea! (do your shaking movement as you let your hands fall down to the floor)
Then there were...one...two...(pause whilst you all find two fingers)
Repeat the rhyme until you have only one jellyfish left.
Now that jellyfish felt lonely all by himself, so he decided to go for a swim too...
No green jellyfish...(hold your fingers in a fist).

Questions to ask
Has anyone seen a jellyfish? (Share your experiences so that all the children have an idea of what a jellyfish is.) Who can hold up five fingers? Shall we try to count them? Hold up ten fingers!

For younger children
Younger children will need a helper beside them to help with the counting movements. If the helper starts with 'one...', the youngest will probably learn to join in with 'two...'.

For older children
Older children love to have a go with the tambourine during the 'warm-up'. Challenge them to count on their fingers up to ten.

Follow-up activities
● Try some other action rhymes which involve counting on fingers such as 'The Three Bears' in *Okki-tokki-unga* (A&C Black).
● When a child has a birthday with you, practise finger counting after you have sung 'Happy Birthday'.

COLOURFUL CIRCLES

Learning objective
To identify and sort colours into sets.

Group size
Six to eight children.

What you need
A selection of small toys and objects each coloured in a shade of red, green, blue or yellow. Four large hoops, one each in red, green, blue and yellow. Alternatively you could use four large sheets of paper in the four colours.

Setting up
Collect together a box full of small toys and objects, all of which are coloured a shade of red, green, blue or yellow. Try to have enough for four or five toys per child.

What to do
Ask the children to sit around in a circle and set the four hoops or sheets of paper in the centre of the circle on the floor. Let the children pass the box of toys around the circle. Invite each of them in turn to look away while putting in a hand and pulling out a toy. Help the child to identify the colour of the toy selected and then to match the colour with the appropriate hoop, placing it inside the hoop. Continue passing the box around giving each child a turn until all the toys have been taken out and matched.

Questions to ask
Do you know what colour that is? Is it the same colour as this hoop or this hoop? If you have a toy in an unusual shade, invite the whole group to decide which hoop to match it with, talking about the differences in shades of the same colour.

For younger children
Sit an adult helper beside the younger children, to prompt the colour name with its first sound if needed, 'It's r...'. Help them to place the toy against the different hoops until they can match the colour.

For older children
Have a few toys which are red and blue or yellow and green and discuss the problem of which hoop to place these toys in. See if you can find a way of overlapping the hoops so that you have a 'red and blue' set.

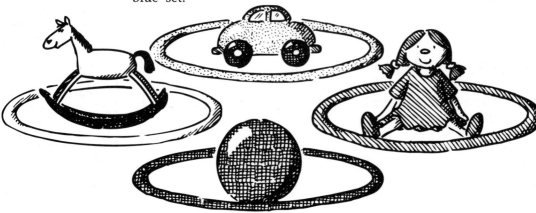

Follow-up activities
● Expand the number of sets by introducing more colours.
● Use paint mixing to make sheets of paper to match more unusual shades and colours.
● Go round the circle and look for examples of the colours in each child's clothing.

MUSICAL NUMBERS

Learning objective
To match and recognize numerals to five.

Group size
Six children.

What you need
Photocopiable sheet on page 60, a cassette recorder and musical tape, drawstring bag.

Setting up
Photocopy the activity sheet twice and cut the numerals out. Mount one set on a strip of card in a number line from one to five. Mount the other set onto individual cards so that each one can be matched directly to the number line. If you laminate the materials they can also be used for other number activities.

What to do
Place the prepared number line on the floor in the centre of the circle, and place the number cards into the drawstring bag. Tell the children that you are going to play some music and they can pass the bag around until the music stops. Ask a helper to operate the cassette recorder. When the music stops, ask the child holding the bag to pull out one number card. *Do you know what number it is?* Help the child match it to the number line. Point with your finger moving from '1' to that number on the number line whilst all the children join in with the counting. Replace the card in the bag and start the music again for the next child's turn.

This is a useful way of moving on from the stage when a child can count by rote but not yet with one-to-one correspondence or with recognition of digits. Because all the children in the circle are helping, the child is not at risk of failing.

Questions to ask
Do you know anyone who is two? Can you count to four on your fingers? Can you count the pictures on your number card? Who can tell me what this number is (point to your number line)?

For younger children
Concentrate on the numbers 1 to 3 only.

For older children
Extend this activity to the numbers 1 to 10.

Follow-up activities
● Use the number line to support other number activities. If a child cannot remember a digit, show the number line, match the digit, and count along the number line together until you reach that number.
● Display a large number line on the wall all the time.
● Match sets of objects to cards with the same digit, placing two cars on a card showing the number 2.

ONE KANGAROO

Learning objective
To practise counting to ten.

Group size
Ten to include any adults.

What you need
Copy of the kangaroo rhyme (below).

Setting up
Familiarize yourself with the rhyme or alternatively sing the song 'One Elephant Went Out to Play' in *Okki-tokki-unga* (A&C Black).

What to do
Sit all the children in a circle, but stand up yourself. Say this rhyme:

One kangaroo goes out to play;
He jumps up high and shouts hurray!
He wants his friends to be there too,
So he calls for another kangaroo.

Bounce around while you say the first line, jump up high for the second, beckon the other children in the third, and choose one to stand up and join you in the last.

Now ask the children to help you count the 'kangaroos'. Place your hand gently on all the heads in turn, starting with your own. Count slowly and with emphasis as you touch each head 'One...two...'.

Repeat the verse:
Two kangaroos go out to play;
They jump up high and shout hurray!
They want their friends to be there too,
So they call for another kangaroo.

Encourage one more 'kangaroo' to join in each verse, stopping to count the heads. When everyone is standing up, change the last two lines:

And when the stars are in the sky
They bounce off home and wave goodbye.

Questions to ask
How many legs has a kangaroo? How many eyes has a kangaroo? Who can jump high? Try counting without touching the heads and find out how much more difficult it becomes.

For younger children
If they are too shy to stand up, still count their heads as they sit in the circle. Ask a helper to encourage them to count 'one, two, three' for the helper to continue. Choose the younger children to be 'kangaroos' first and they can be fully involved from the start, in the centre of the circle, while the older children continue to count.

For older children
Challenge the older children to count on their fingers as you count the 'kangaroos'.

Follow-up activities
● Look for opportunities for the children to count each other, such as when you are choosing the right size group for a 'circle time' activity.
● Share other rhymes which can involve counting the children such as 'Five Currant Buns' or 'Five Little Speckled Frogs' (traditional).
● Challenge the children to point to a number card representing the number of children. Start with numbers up to five and extend to ten.

HOW WARM YOU ARE!

Learning objective
To carry out instructions relating to position.

Group size
Eight to ten children.

What you need
A woolly hat, a box with lid, a doll's bed with cover, a shopping bag which cannot be seen through, an anorak, a rug, a small teddy bear. A second helper.

Setting up
Place everything except the teddy bear on the floor at different locations outside the circle but easily in view.

What to do
Ask the helper to move out of sight and sound of the circle, and then tell the children that you are going to hide the teddy bear in one of six places. While the children watch from the circle, move round the hat, anorak, box, bag, rug and bed, placing the bear inside or under each object in turn.

Tell the children what you are doing, emphasizing the position word, 'Look...I *could* hide Teddy *under* the bed'. Ask for ideas and hide the teddy bear in one of the places. Call your helper back in and say that the bear is hidden under or inside (whichever is so) something. As the helper moves round, the children can sing:
How warm you are, how warm you are,
How warm you are, how warm...
to the tune of 'Auld Lang Syne', singing louder as the helper moves close to the correct hiding place, and singing quieter as the helper moves away.

Once the teddy bear is found, one of the children can be the finder, moving out of the room with the helper while the other children decide on the next hiding place.

Questions to ask
Did the singing help you find the bear? Where else could we have put the bear? Who can put the bear on top of/at the side of/in front of/behind the hat? Ask 'where' questions relating to pairs of objects around the room and encourage the children to find the correct position word.

For younger children
Have three hiding places inside the circle, and encourage the children to cover their eyes while you quickly slip the bear inside or under one of them.

For older children
Hide the teddy bear anywhere in the room (not necessarily in specific hiding places) telling the child that he is on top of/under/behind something. As before sing the song to guide them.

Follow-up activities
● When playing with construction toys and small world toys, talk to the child about positions and ask 'where?' questions.
● Provide a selection of six objects and challenge a child to place one in/on/under/behind/in front of/beside another. Start with one or two objects and positions and build up once the child is learning successfully.

TEDDY BEAR, TEDDY BEAR

Learning objective
To use words to describe positions.

Group size
Up to 20 children.

What you need
The rhyme (below).

Setting up
Familiarize yourself with the rhyme shown below.

What to do
Gather the children in a circle and chant this rhyme together. Invite the children to stand up and join in the actions.

Teddy bear, teddy bear, turn around,
Teddy bear, teddy bear, touch the ground,
Teddy bear, teddy bear, reach up high,
Teddy bear, teddy bear, say 'goodbye'.

Now let the children take it in turns to pretend to be the teddy bear in the centre of the circle while the other children sit down and sing.

Finally, invite the children to tell the teddy bear what to do, 'Turn around!', 'Sit down', 'Put your arms up'.

Questions to ask
Are my hands up/down/in front of me/behind me? What other position words do you know? Can you put your feet underneath you? Who can put their hands on top of their heads?

For younger children
Say the rhyme together and do the actions only.

For older children
Make up some more verses for your song together (don't worry if these do not rhyme) and practise the actions together.

Follow-up activities
● Pretend to be a robot and let the children tell you what to do, 'Turn round', 'Sit down'.
● Line up the children and practise using positional vocabulary.
● Use your positional words at 'tidy-up time' to tell the children where things belong.
● Learn some other action rhymes which use positional words such as 'Five Little Froggies' in *This Little Puffin* compiled by Elizabeth Matterson (Puffin).

FOLLOW THAT

Learning objective
To continue a sequence of shapes.

Group size
Four to six children.

What you need
Coloured card, shallow box.

Setting up
Cut out a selection of shapes (each approximately 10 cm across) from coloured card to provide ten circles, ten squares and ten triangles. All the circles should be one colour, all the squares a second colour, and all the triangles a third colour. Laminate the shapes and also use them for other mathematical activities. Place all the shapes in a shallow box where they can be easily seen and sorted through.

What to do
Gather the children in a circle on the floor. Tell them that you are going to make a pattern with some shapes. Start by placing six circles in a line and invite each child in turn to choose a shape to continue the same pattern (ie all circles). Continue until all the correct shapes in the box are used up. Next, try placing circles and squares alternately for six shapes and again invite the children in turn to choose the next shape. Think of some other simple sequences for the children to continue.

Questions to ask
Do you know the names of these shapes? Can you carry on a spoken pattern? – 'one, two, one, two...'. What patterns can you see when you look around? (Repeating railings or fence posts, paving squares, alternate windows and walls around the playroom, cars parked in a row and so on.)

For younger children
Keep to simple sequences: a row of triangles or a row of squares. If the child reaches for an incorrect shape, point to the correct choice and then praise the child for choosing it.

For older children
Start some more complicated sequences: two triangles and one square (repeated) or a circle, a square and a triangle (repeated). Invite the children to start their own sequences for others to continue.

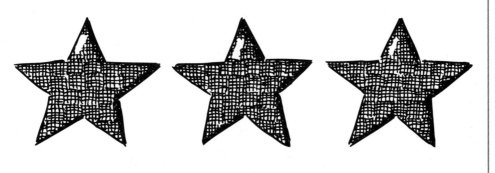

Follow-up activities
● Make an activity sheet for each child with a simple pattern (a wavy line or a zigzag) or sequence for them to continue with a pencil.
● Thread beads in a given sequence, encouraging the children to continue the pattern you have started.
● Use coloured peg boards to repeat sequences and two-dimensional patterns.
● Cut out sticky paper shapes and help the children to make a frieze with a repeating pattern all around the room.

HOW OLD ARE YOU?

Learning objective
To explore numbers to five by counting, identifying and naming numerals.

Group size
Up to ten children.

What you need
Photocopiable page 60, a card with each child's name on, Blu-Tack.

Setting up
Copy page 60 and laminate (or use the laminated number cards already prepared for 'Musical Numbers' on page 21). Place the five numerals side by side and in order, about 30 centimetres apart, in the centre of the circle. Place the name cards randomly, name side up.

What to do
Gather the children in a circle on the floor. Point to the numbers and invite the children to tell you what they are, starting with 1 and moving up to 5. Now challenge them to tell you what number you are pointing at in a random order. Then invite individual children to come forward and point to the number which you name for them and to tell you the name of a number that you point to.

These warm-up activities will serve to remind the children of the numbers they have been learning.

Tell the children that you would like to know how old they are. Help the children to take it in turns to find their own name card and to place it under the number which represents their age. When they have each had a turn help them count how many names you have in each category. Find a way of recording your results semi-permanently such as by mounting the cards on the wall with Blu-Tack.

Questions to ask
Can you tell, just by looking at the cards, how old most of you are? What would we see if we did this in a year's time? How many candles did you have on your cake last year? Show me the number which shows how old your little brother is. (If the children insist, be prepared for an 'over 21' category for yourself!)

For younger children
Keep the group size small, and only use the number cards which actually reflect the children's ages.

For older children
Help them complete a simple histogram graph using coloured sticky squares and columns to record their results. Talk about what you are doing so that the children can interpret their results simply.

Follow-up activities
● Look for other facts to record in a similar way. Who likes orange squash and who likes milk? Who has long hair and who has short hair?
● Make a wall chart with ages across the top and names and birthdays beneath.
● Talk about growing and changing; what can you do now which you will not be able to do when you are older (and vice-versa)?

CHAPTER THREE

PERSONAL AND SOCIAL DEVELOPMENT

Help children get to know each other and develop confidence within the circle with these ideas to encourage turn-taking and feeling positive about oneself. There are also opportunities to talk about many cultures and to recognize feelings and expressions.

FRIENDSHIP RING

Learning objective
To get to know everyone's name.

Group size
Eight children.

What you need
A big teddy bear, rag doll, or equivalent.

Setting up
Clear a space so that you can all hold hands and dance in a ring.

What to do
Start by sitting down and singing a 'Hello song' to everybody in the circle, mentioning them by name. Sing the 'Hello song' to the tune of 'Tommy Thumb, Tommy Thumb, Where are you?' from *This Little Puffin* compiled by Elizabeth Matterson (Puffin) but substitute the child's own name.

Hello Katie, Hello Katie,
Where are you?
Here I am! Here I am!
How do you do?

Now introduce the teddy bear/doll to everybody in the circle. Make it move around the circle shaking each child's hand in turn and saying 'How do you do, (child's name)?' Suggest that you include Teddy in a dance. Stand up and all hold hands, with you 'helping' Teddy to join the ring. Dance round to 'Ring-o-Ring-o-Roses':

Ring-o-Ring-o-Roses, a pocket full of posies,
Atishoo, Atishoo, we all fall down!

Stand up again and give the bear to a child, mentioning them by name. They can then take a turn in dancing Teddy round the ring. Between turns, ask each child to 'Please give the bear to (another child's name)' so that the children begin to identify each other by name. Thank each child by name for doing so.

When everyone has had a turn, say that Teddy has forgotten their names. Make him approach each child in turn, and encourage all the children to call out that child's name.

Questions to ask
Why do we have names? What are the names of people in your family? Does anyone else in your family have the same name as you?

For younger children
Keep the group size to three or four children.

For older children
Older children will cope with a larger group, and will be confident enough to 'dance' Teddy in the centre of the ring.

Follow-up activities
● Make some laminated name cards (see page 26) and use them to mark places in your 'circle time' occasionally; ask the children to find their own name.
● Use the children's names when you are addressing them, to gain their attention and make your communication special to them.
● Make colourful name badges to wear in your group so that all adult helpers can address each child by their name.

I LIKE YOU

Learning objective
To build up positive
self-esteem.

Group size
Six children.

What you need
One piece of artwork, model or other creation made by each child.

Setting up
Wait until you know the children and their families reasonably well before doing this activity. In addition to the children's artwork, which you are going to show off and praise to the other children, make a point of finding out about the children's likes and interests at home from parents. You are aiming to find something special and positive to say about each child.

What to do
Gather the children in a circle. Praise them for all the hard work they have been doing recently. Show the examples of the children's work and point out all the positive aspects of each piece. Then say something positive about each child in the group: how kind they have been to their granny, how they help to look after the family pet, or how hard they have been trying at football.

Finally, move round the circle talking about one child at a time, inviting the other children to say why they like her or him. Encourage the children to make positive comments about each other. If children begin to make negative statements, remind them that you are talking about liking people and being kind.

Questions to ask
What do you like about this model? Wasn't this a good idea? Who else is helpful at home? What do you do when you are being helpful?

For younger children
Younger children will find it easiest to talk about concrete things: liking the way another child looks, or liking their shoes.

For older children
Encourage older children to think in a wider sense: liking the way another child behaves or sharing an interest.

Follow-up activities
● Invite the parents to a special display of work which the children are proud of, making sure that each child has a piece included.
● Use a home-school diary to use with parents, so you can keep up to date with news from home.
● Look for any opportunities to place certain children together as play partners based on the things you have learned about each of the children.

PASSING SMILES

Learning objective
To recognize and copy facial expressions.

Group size
Up to eight children.

What you need
A hand-held mirror for use with younger children.

Setting up
Gather the children in a circle, sitting on the floor.

What to do
Start by making a smiling face yourself. Ask the children if they think you are happy or sad. Now make a frowning face. Ask the children how you look. Try a surprised face and a sad face. Now look worried or frightened. Talk about feelings and facial expressions and invite the children to copy each expression that you make.

Now tell the children that you are going to play a game passing a smile all the way round the circle. First smile at your neighbour and encourage the child to smile back. Then encourage that child to pass the smile on to the next child until that child smiles back. Gradually pass the smile all the way round the circle.

Repeat this game with different expressions, passing a sad face, a cross face or a frightened face round. Finish with passing a smile around the circle again.

Questions to ask
When you smile, does it make you feel happy inside? How did it feel when you all looked sad? If someone smiles at you, how does it feel? If someone looks sad, what does it make you want to do? Talk about how smiling can make other people feel happy too.

For younger children
Pass a hand-held mirror round so that younger children can practise making the expressions.

For older children
Begin to talk about things which make you feel happy, sad, frightened, cross, surprised.

Follow-up activities
● Dance to some 'happy' and 'sad' music.
● Paint 'happy' and 'sad' pictures for a wall display.
● Play a guessing game: make an expression and ask the children to guess how you are feeling today.
● When you see individual children looking sad or cross, help them to put those feelings into words and show that you recognize how they are feeling.

LUCY LOCKET

Learning objective
To join in a circle game with confidence.

Group size
Up to 15 children.

What you need
A pocket handkerchief or scarf. An additional adult helper.

Setting up
You will need to do this activity on a carpeted area so that the children do not slip when they move quickly. The children should wear plimsolls or have bare feet.

What to do
Sit in a circle and introduce the game. Start by asking an adult helper to be 'Lucy'. The helper moves around the outside of the circle, holding the pocket handkerchief, whilst everyone else sings this song to the tune of 'Yankee Doodle'.

Lucy Locket lost her pocket,
Kitty Fisher found it,
Not a penny was there in it,
But a ribbon round it!

The helper then drops the handkerchief behind a child and continues to move round the circle. Call the child's name and encourage them to get up, pick up the handkerchief and chase 'Lucy' with it before she returns to sit in the space that the child has left in the circle. That child becomes 'Lucy' next time. Ask your helper to remain standing and help the children. You can help by prompting the chasers by name. Continue until everyone has had a turn.

As an alternative try playing the game with a heavy beanbag, encouraging 'Lucy' to drop it behind the circle while all the children sit quietly with their eyes closed. Ask if they can hear it fall and if they can tell who it is behind.

Questions to ask
Do you know what a 'penny' is? I wonder what Lucy Locket's 'pocket' was? How did you know it was your turn? Could you hear the handkerchief fall?

For younger children
When a much younger child is 'Lucy', ask the helper to move round the circle holding the child's hand.

For older children
See if they can join in without prompting, simply by remaining alert and watching out for when and where the handkerchief falls.

Follow-up activities
● Talk about 'old fashioned' money and bring some in to show the children how heavy it was.
● Make a wall collage of Lucy Locket and her 'pocket'.
● Make paper 'pockets' (or envelopes) for the children to take home or keep a special drawing or treasure in. Decorate them with lace and ribbons.

HOW DO YOU DO?

Learning objective
To introduce a friend and begin to think what it is like to be someone else.

Group size
Ten or 12; an even number.

What you need
No special materials are required for this activity.

What to do
Gather the children together in a circle. Call one of your helpers over, shake hands and say, 'How do you do? I'm (your own name), what's your name?'. Ask the children if they know why grown-ups sometimes shake hands. Talk about greetings in different cultures: a hug, a kiss on the cheek, a bow. Now practise shaking hands in the circle, by passing a handshake all around the ring as you did in the activity 'Passing smiles' on page 29. Use some of the other greetings too.

Help the children find partners, and make sure that they are sitting next to their partners in the circle. Tell each child that that you are going to help them introduce their partner. They should say what their name is and what things they like best. Give an example by introducing your helper, 'This is Tara, she likes singing songs and eating lots of strawberries'. Give the children a minute or so to ask their partner questions and move around the circle to ensure that each child knows what to say.

Take it in turns to go round the circle, letting each child introduce their partners, saying something about them to the rest of the group.

Questions to ask
Help the children find the right questions to ask their partners. What is your name? What is your favourite thing to eat? What do you like on television? What is your favourite toy? Encourage them to think about what it is like to be the other person.

For younger children
Sit a helper beside younger children to help with this activity and to make sure they are completely involved.

For older children
Encourage them to ask several questions so that they can talk about their neighbour in more detail.

Follow-up activities
● Introduce visitors to the group with a handshake and include the children when you are exchanging names so that they feel valued and included.
● Make a big poster entitled 'How do you do?' introducing people who help in the community: a picture of a lollipop person, a teacher or a police officer.
● Sing a song as you shake hands in the circle (to the tune of 'Here we go round the mulberry bush'): This is the way we shake our hands... saying 'How do you do?' in the morning.

ROUNDABOUT TURNS

Learning objective
To wait and take turns within a group.

Group size
Six children.

What you need
Copy photocopiable activity sheet on page 61 to provide a roundabout pony for each child to colour and cut out. A selection of colouring crayons or pens, scissors, a pencil, a board, modelling clay, four cotton reels, a large dice, shaking beaker and bowl.

Setting up
Make the base for a roundabout from a circle of card 50 cm in diameter divided into sections and coloured brightly, and assemble it with the cotton reels, clay and pencils as shown below:

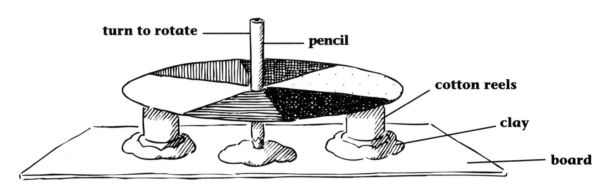

turn to rotate —— pencil

cotton reels

clay

board

What to do
Start this activity at a table, helping the children to colour and cut out their roundabout horses. When they are complete fold them across the middle so that they will stand up.

Remove the large circle of card from the roundabout and ask the children to help you colour in the segments. Work together co-operatively, colouring in one segment each. As you work, talk together about fairgrounds and roundabouts.

Now gather the children in your circle, inviting each to bring their roundabout pony. Place the coloured circle back on the roundabout and place it in the centre. Tell the children that you are going to play a game about taking turns. Encourage each child in turn to shake the dice in the beaker and empty it into the bowl (this prevents the dice from getting lost). If a child throws a 'one', then their pony can take up a place on the roundabout. Once a child has placed their pony, they no longer take a turn at throwing the dice. Continue until all the ponies are on the roundabout, then turn it around for the children to see.

Questions to ask
When is it important to take turns in the group? What would happen if you didn't? Can you think of other ways in which you take turns? (Queuing for the slide, having one go each with the tractor, taking a ticket when you arrive in a busy shoe shop.) Did you have to count the 'one' on the dice, or did you know straight away what it was? What about the 'three', or the 'six'?

Follow-up activities
● Make a fairground scene out of found materials with stalls, big wheel, helter-skelter, roller-coaster and roundabout. Play a tape of fairground music as you show it off to parents and visitors.
● Construct a simple obstacle course, and practise forming a queue and following each other in turn over the course.
● Praise the children for turn-taking and sharing throughout your sessions.

WE'RE OK!

Learning objective
To develop a positive self-image.

Group size
Individuals; group of six to eight children.

What you need
For each child, a selection of artwork and models, together with other evidence and records of achievement (photographic records, wall friezes to which the child has contributed, shared memories).

Setting up
Towards the end of term, gather together some of the children's work which has not yet gone home. This becomes easier if you have been collecting it in individual portfolios. Look back through the children's records of achievement so that you can help each child to recall all that you have done together that term.

What to do
Find time to sit with each child for five minutes and look through their work together, talking about all the different ways in which they have contributed to the group that term.

The purpose of this activity is to help each child thier personal remember achievements, feel positive about their contributions, feel valued within the group, and to begin to review their own progress and plans. Make sure this is a very positive experience for both of you; if there are particular doubts about the children's behaviour or conduct, this is not the moment to talk about them. Look instead for signs of effort and improvement which you can praise. Now ask each child to choose the pieces of work or share a memory about which they are most proud.

Invite each child to bring their chosen piece of work or memory to 'circle time' and encourage the children, one by one, to 'show and tell' it to all the others.

Questions to ask
Why were you so pleased with this picture? (Share your pleasure too, and say exactly what it is that *you* like about it.) Would you like to do more finger painting next term? Will you do your train tracks differently next time? If so, do you know how? How would you like to make your models even better? Once in the circle, help the other children ask questions and say what it is that they liked about it too.

For younger children
Keep the discussion very concrete by looking and talking about the creations which the child has made. Find out what they like doing best in the group and talk about how you can do more of the same work next term.

For older children
Help the child evaluate their work more reflectively. Which bits of this do you like best? Which parts would you change? How?

Follow-up activities
● Help each child plan what they would like to do during a session and then evaluate with you how it went.
● Include the child's comments about their work in any end-of-term report.
● Make an art gallery of each child's favourite creations. Encourage parents to look at this regularly, and make sure each child has chosen something to be displayed there.

ALL ONE WORLD

Learning objective
To talk about children from a range of cultures and countries and explore related objects and possessions.

Group size
Up to 12 children.

What you need
Visitors from your local community with artefacts to show.

Setting up
'Circle time' is an ideal opportunity for finding out about one another and sharing. Invite visitors from your local community to meet the children and to bring in a collection of artefacts, food, clothing, utensils, books and pictures from a range of cultures, faiths and communities to share with the children, so that they can ask questions and find out more about their local community and the world around them. Start with local contacts whom you already know: a parent or grandparent of one of your children, a local faith leader, somebody from your committee or local council. Think ahead of the range of cultures, faiths and communities reflected in your neighbourhood and set up a series of visits.

What to do
Gather the children in a circle and provide a chair for your visitor within the circle. Go round the group so that each person can introduce themselves. Now give your visitor time to talk to the children and to pass round artefacts or other items for the children to handle and explore. These might include some fabric or garments, different breads or exotic fruits, spices to smell, a musical instrument, a religious artefact, a tool, a photograph, a piece of pottery or ornament. Use your knowledge of the children to keep the discussion simple, to ensure that the children understand and to help them join in.

Questions to ask
Help the children to frame questions for your visitor. Ask the children questions about what they are handling to help them use all their senses. What does it feel like? Do you like the taste? What does the smell remind you of? Ask your own questions to the visitor to add to the children's understanding, keeping the information relevant from the children's point of view.

For younger children
Keep the group small and base the talk around objects or food which the children can handle or taste.

For older children
You will be able to make your discussion more abstract. Talk about ways of life, different faiths and different ways of doing things.

Follow-up activities
● Make a display of items for the children to talk about and explore.
● Paint pictures or create models linked to the talking you have done during 'circle time'.
● Arrange for a visit to a local place of worship, a local restaurant or a cultural centre linked to your visitor.

CHAPTER FOUR

Develop the children's knowledge and understanding of the world around them with these activities to help them think about and explore animals, families and homes, and the natural world. Encourage thought about the questions we ask, and how to look more closely at similarities and differences around us.

OLD MACDONALD'S ZOO

Learning objective
To link animal sounds and actions.

Group size
Whole group.

What you need
No specific materials are needed. Arrange for a musical accompaniment if you have a musician among your staff or helpers.

Setting up
Find out about the country of origin, habitat and diets of zoo animals with which the children will be familiar.

What to do
Gather the children in a circle and tell them that you are going to sing a special version of 'Old Macdonald's Farm' called 'Old Macdonald's Zoo'. Warn them that you are going to ask them soon for ideas of the animals that Old Macdonald might keep in a zoo.

Old Macdonald had a zoo, E–I–E–I–O,
And on that zoo, he had a ...

At this point, stop the song and seek suggestions from the children. Accept one child's idea, and then ask the whole group for ideas for an action and a sound to go with that zoo animal, perhaps a 'tiger'.

With a roar roar here, and a roar roar there,
Here a roar, there a roar, everywhere a roar roar,
Old Macdonald had a zoo, E–I–E–I–O.

Continue for several verses, choosing a different child's suggestion for each verse. Let the chorus build up cumulatively each time, by adding the previous animal's sounds to the new.

Questions to ask
What sound does a snake make? How does it move? Can we make an action like that to go with the song? Where do snakes live; is it always in a zoo? What do they like to eat? Who has seen a snake? Use your questions to build on the children's knowledge and understanding of the natural world.

For younger children
Talk about zoos first and help the children think of an animal by looking through a picture book with you.

For older children
Introduce some more unusual animals to the children, sharing pictures and information about their natural habitats. Talk about zoos, and the dangers that some animals have in their habitats. Introduce the idea of caring carefully for creatures in our natural world.

Follow-up activities
● Make up other versions of this song: 'Old Macdonald had a Pet Shop', 'Old Macdonald had a Wood', 'Old Macdonald had a Pond' for example.
● Paint and stick a giant frieze or collage to show all the animals that Old Macdonald had.
● Encourage the children to think of their own verses and actions for other rhymes they know such as 'The Wheels on the Bus', *This Little Puffin* compiled by Elizabeth Matterson (Puffin).

MY FAMILY

Learning objective
To talk about families and where we live.

Group size
Small groups, then a circle of ten children.

What you need
Sheets of paper and a selection of paints and brushes.

Setting up
Set up an area for painting, and prepare a large wall frieze of coloured paper ready to display the finished paintings. Have each child's home address at hand so that you can help them to remember it.

What to do
Encourage the children to each paint a picture of their home along with the people and pets who live there, painted outside the house. Remain sensitive to individual children's domestic circumstances. Indeed, some children might like to paint two homes if they have more than one set of parents and step-parents.

Ask each child for the names of each family member and write these in. Label each painting: (Child's name) lives at (Child's house number and street). Hang the paintings to dry until later in the session or until the next time you meet.

Gather the children in a circle and talk about different homes and families. Ask the children in turn to show their pictures, try to remember where they live, and introduce all the family members in their picture.

Finally, mount the children's pictures on the frieze to look like a big street or village.

Questions to ask
Use your questions to show the range of homes and families so that no one feels left out or different. Ask the children about the differrent types of houses: some may live in terraces of houses, some in flats, some over a shop, some in the countryside, some in towns, some in villages. Talk about families: sometimes there is one grown-up, sometimes two, sometimes grandparents too, sometimes lots of children and sometimes no others. Some of us have more than one family and home.

For younger children
Draw the outline of a house with big windows. Ask the child to 'draw' a member of their family in each window. If necessary draw in the face and encourage the child to add the features.

For older children
Draw a big map of the local area and use coloured stickers to mark where each child lives.

Follow-up activities
● Talk about the local area and the main buildings there: the shops, places of worship, the library, hotels, factories and so on. What happens in each place?
● Invite children to bring in family photographs and make a display.
● Help each child put together a scrap-book made of A4-size sugar paper of 'My Family' to include paintings, mark-making, writing that they have dictated to you, photographs and cut out items.

TREASURE CHEST

Learning objective
To explore a selection of made and natural objects.

Group size
Up to 12 children.

What you need
A large box (if possible looking like a treasure chest), a selection of made and natural objects, so that there is at least one per child. These might include: a piece of pottery, a piece of driftwood, a feather, a small painting in a frame, a string of beads, an interesting stone, a fossil, a piece of shiny or colourful fabric, a dried seed-head, a pine cone, a carved piece of wood, a metallic ornament, an unusual musical instrument, a shell, a natural sponge, a small book, a plastic toy, a loofah, a twig and a bar of soap. Provide an equal number of natural and made objects, and make sure each one is interesting to feel, to look at, to listen to or to smell.

Setting up
Place all the objects together in the box and close the lid.

What to do
Gather the children in the circle and invite each child in turn to take one object out of the treasure chest and to pass it around the circle so that each child can explore it. Now ask the children to tell you as much as they can about it. Put that object to one side.

Continue until each child has had a turn at choosing the object. After the activity, put all the objects on a table for the children to inspect and to show their parents.

Questions to ask
Use your questions to encourage the children to use all their senses when exploring the object. What does it look like? Does it have a sound or a smell? Ask questions which offer the children a choice of describing words. Is it heavy or light, shiny or dull, strong or delicate? Finally, ask the children whether they think that the object has been made by someone, or whether it is part of nature. Encourage the children to wonder and share pleasure at beauty and detail.

For younger children
Keep the objects simple and familiar. Encourage the children to think of one thing to say about each object.

For older children
Introduce some artefacts from a wide range of cultures and origins, such as a piece of lava rock, soapstone or a desert rose. Find out a little about the objects you choose so that you can tell the children more about them. Encourage the children to be more imaginative in their descriptions – providing as much detail as possible.

Follow-up activities
● Use the objects to encourage the children to sort into 'natural' and 'made' objects on the display table.
● Go on a discovery walk and add to your collection.
● Encourage parents to talk with their children about natural and made objects, and to help their child find one of each to bring in to the group.

THE BUILDING SONG

Learning objective
To think about and mime the skills needed in building a house.

Group size
Eight to 12 children.

What you need
The photocopiable activity sheet on page 62 which shows a set of illustrations showing some of the stages in building a house. Children's information book showing different stages in photographs.

Setting up
Photocopy one activity sheet for each child.

What to do
Gather the children in a circle and talk about building a house, showing any books and photographs you have available. Pass round an activity sheet for each child to look at. Ask the children to think of ways of miming the different trades: laying the bricks, hammering the nails, soldering the pipework and so on. Now sing the following words to the traditional tune of 'Here we go Round the Mulberry Bush':

This is the way we build a house...
This is the way we dig down deep...
This is the way we lay the bricks/tile the roof/paint the walls and so on.

Invite the children to add actions to go with the song. Perhaps one child could be a builder, one a plumber and one an electrician.

Move to a table and let the children colour in the sheet. Encourage them to talk about what they can see in the pictures as they do so.

Questions to ask
Look around your own building and ask questions to encourage the children to think about how it was put together.

For younger children
Say the rhyme for the children as they hammer in time to the rhythm of your words.

For older children
Pass round a selection of tools, including a mallet, a plumb line and a spirit level. Ask the children who might use each tool and for what.

Follow-up activities
● Use construction sets to build houses, placing them together to make an estate or street.
● Arrange for the children to watch and talk to a visiting joiner, plumber or builder while they work. Observe all safety precautions necessary.
● Use a sponge to print brick shapes on a wall ready onto which you can mount a painted 'Humpty Dumpty'.

WHY? WHAT? WHEN?

Learning objective
To practise questioning and answering.

Group size
Eight to ten children.

What you need
A glove puppet and a picture book, such as *The Very Hungry Caterpillar* by Eric Carle (Hamish Hamilton).

Setting up
In this example *The Very Hungry Caterpillar* has been chosen, but you can adapt the activity to suit any picture book. Read through the story book to yourself and think ahead of the questions you will use for this activity.

What to do
Gather the children in a circle for a story. Introduce the puppet to the group and explain that he often gets a bit muddled up when he is asking questions, ask if the children will help him. Read one page of your chosen book at a time to the group, sharing the pictures with the children and the puppet. At the end of each page, ask the puppet whether it has got any questions. Then make it speak, asking 'what?', 'where?', 'why?' and 'when?' questions, but getting the questions muddled up.

For example:
Read the first page of *The Very Hungry Caterpillar*. The puppet then asks 'Why is the moon?' Encourage the children to shake their heads. Can they think of a better question for the puppet to ask about the moon? With their help, the puppet asks 'Where is the moon?' or 'What is the moon?' and the children think of helpful answers.

In later pages, the children help the puppet ask 'When?' questions about all the food which the caterpillar eats.

Questions to ask
Encourage the children to sound out their questions so that they can listen to them and decide which questions work: 'Why is a caterpillar? When is a caterpillar? What is a caterpillar?' Ask the children to think about question words and the kinds of answers they provide. Talk about the importance of asking questions to find things out.

For younger children
Keep the examples simple, with the children always having to change the puppet's 'Why?' question to a 'What?' question.

For older children
Let them take turns in speaking for the puppet so that they can invent nonsense questions of their own.

Follow-up activities
● Hide a toy in a bag and let the children ask questions to find out what you have hidden.
● Make a giant collage in the shape of a question mark, add 'what?', 'when?', 'where?', 'why?' and 'how?'.
● In your parents' newsletter, discuss the importance of answering children's questions.

WHEN I WAS ONE

Learning objective
To think about growing up, from babyhood to school age.

Group size
Six children.

What you need
Some photographs of each child, a large envelope for each child with their names on the front, a comfortable carpeted area.

Setting up
Ask parents to help you by supplying some photographs of their children and writing the children's name and age at the time of the picture on the reverse.

What to do
When the children arrive with their photographs, place them into the prepared envelopes. Put these on one side until you are ready to start the activity.

Ask the children to kneel down in a circle, and pass round their photographs. Tell them that you are going to talk about growing up. Who has a photograph of themselves as a tiny baby? Who has a photograph of themselves as a one-year-old? Repeat for each age. Pass the photographs round, as you talk about growing up and as you share memories and experiences.

Questions to ask
What kind of care does a new baby need? What can you do now which a baby can't? What things did you learn to do when you were one? Can you find a photograph of yourself crawling? Why do babies need to cry a lot? What can you do now which you won't be able to do when you are a grown-up?

For younger children
Keep the group small and ask parents to write a few details about the photograph on the reverse for you to talk about with the child.

For older children
Use a flip chart or whiteboard and draw simple pictures showing all the developmental stages that children move through from birth to five years old: crawling, shaking rattles, talking, running, scribbling, building bricks, painting, putting on clothes, feeding themselves, writing their name and so on.

Follow-up activities
● Read and talk about the picture book *When I was Little* by Marcia Williams (Walker Books).
● Mount the baby photographs on a wall and encourage the children to guess who's who.
● Make simple timelines for each child's set of photos, showing the progression from birth to three.
● Arrange a visit from a parent with a baby or a one-year-old, complete with their favourite toys and special equipment for looking after them: a bottle, a nappy or a toddler toy.

FOLD AND FOLD AGAIN

Learning objective
To practise folding skills.

Group size
Ten to 12 children.

What you need
A large double sheet of newspaper for each child and plenty of space for your circle, with a floor surface which is not slippery. A cassette recorder and a tape suitable for slow plodding movement.

Setting up
This circle activity is best done in a large space such as a hall. Spread each sheet of paper out to its full spread in the shape of a circle, just one child-sized pace apart. Set up the cassette recorder at the side of the room with an additional helper to operate it. Ensure that the children are wearing plimsolls or trainers.

What to do
Tell the children that they are going to play a 'stepping stones' game, and explain that, when they hear the music, they should step across the newspapers, trying not to put their feet on the floor. Give them a demonstration first. Say that they should move slowly and carefully because the game is going to get more and more difficult!

Start the music and encourage the children to move steadily around the circle. When the music stops, encourage each child to stop on a sheet of their own. Now tell the children to step onto the floor and to fold their sheet of paper exactly into two. This is very difficult for some children and you will need to move round at first showing them what you want them to do.

The game continues with the children folding the sheet of paper one more time each time the music stops, and with you making the circle smaller and smaller. It ends when you all end up stepping onto the floor because the sheets are folded so small!

Questions to ask
Who can fold carefully so that all the corners come together? When do we need to fold things? (Talk about letters, folding up clothes, folding bundles of cloth to transport them.) Who can balance on one leg?

For younger children
Play with a smaller group of children, enlist extra help and support the children individually.

For older children
Challenge the children by starting with smaller sheets of newspaper.

Follow-up activities
● Practise folding sheets of paper into two and four as part of a letter-posting activity.
● Make symmetrical pictures using ink and folding the paper in half.
● Use folding in craft work to make butterfly wings or chains of paper dolls.

SNAP!

Learning objective
To look closely at similarities and differences.

Group size
Up to six children.

What you need
A set of 'Snap!' picture cards and a carpeted area.

Setting up
You can make your own set of cards by creating a set of 36 laminated cards, with six identical sets of designs. In this way, you can adapt the game to suit your children and their levels of capability, using larger and simpler designs for younger children and using more detail which has to be carefully perused for older children.

What to do
Gather the children in a circle on the floor. Talk about 'same' and 'different'. Who is wearing the same colour as Sam? Who is wearing a different colour? Which two children have the same names? Are the children different ages?

Tell the children you are going to play a game using picture cards which are the same or different. Ask them to watch but not touch as you shuffle and deal the cards out, an equal number to each child and placed in a heap in front of each child, picture side down. Tell the children that they must not look at the pictures just yet. One at a time, they must put their top card on top of a central stack, picture side up. If it is the same as the card that is there already, then the children should call 'Snap!' The two cards which are the same are then removed from the game and placed in a heap, picture side up, to one side.

This version of the game is non-competitive, and you will eventually end up with all your pictures sorted into neat sets ready to reshuffle and deal for the next game.

Questions to ask
Why are these cards the same? Why are these two cards different? Can you find me another one that is the same? Who has the same colour eyes? Are your shoes different? Use questions to teach the meaning of 'same' and 'different': these can be very difficult concepts for young children.

For younger children
Keep the designs very different: flowers, bears, cars, suns and so on.

For older children
Make a set of cards with only subtle differences which have to be very carefully perused, such as sets of clowns with different numbers of pom-poms, people with different styles of hat and houses with different shapes of window.

Follow-up activities
● Have a sorting table with two hoops and a selection of objects. Help the children sort objects which are the same and objects which are different.
● Draw a big poster with two similar pictures and challenge the children to find five simple differences between them.
● Use 'same' and 'different' in your craft and collage work by inviting the children to find you another the same or different to a given example.

CHAPTER FIVE

Develop children's physical skills in 'circle time' by aiming and controlling a ball, improving balance skills and learning to co-ordinate their bodies. There are activities for copying actions and movements, and using the space around in a variety of new ways.

LOOBY LOU

What you need

Learning objective
To copy actions and begin to recognize 'right' and 'left'.

Group size
Any size; one helper to four children.

Wide space for this activity, a coloured ribbon or wrist band for each child, and the song 'Here we go Looby Lou', *Okki-tokki-unga* (A&C Black) or in *This Little Puffin* compiled by Elizabeth Matterson (Puffin).

Setting up

Familiarize yourself with this action song.

What to do

Gather the children in a circle, standing up. Ask if anyone knows which is their right hand, if so ask them to hold it up. Ask your helpers to go round the circle helping the children identify their right hands. Give each child a ribbon or wristband and help them to put it on their right wrists. Have three or four practices at holding up the right hand and then the left hand, reminding the children that the ribbon is on their right.

Now challenge the children to waggle their left foot, touch their right knee, cover their left eye and so on. Ask your helpers to encourage and help the children near to them. When you feel the children are ready, start the action song.

Join hands in a circle as you move round singing the chorus. Stop in your places as you sing the verses, making up your own as you go along. Here is an example:
Put your right hand in,
Put your right hand out,
Shake it a little, a little,
and turn yourself about.

Questions to ask

Can anyone close their eyes and hold up their right hand? Now open your eyes; is it the hand with the ribbon on? Who draws pictures with their left hand? Who uses their right hand? Take your shoes off and mix them up: do you know which foot to put them back onto?

For younger children

Keep the size of the group small, with no more than six children and two adults.

For older children

Try to do the action song without using the ribbons. Invent more complicated versions such as asking the children to put their right hand on their left knee.

Follow-up activities
● Help children sort out right and left shoes by inviting parents to place a small dot of paint or liquid paper on the inside of each shoe to match together.
● Always make sure you provide a selection of right- and left-handed scissors when doing craft work.
● Spend two or three minutes on your right and left quiz (above) each week during 'circle time'.

MERRILY WE ROLL ALONG

Learning objective
To aim and catch a
rolling ball.

Group size
Ten children.

What you need
A large ball.

What to do
Gather the children in a circle sitting on the floor with their legs in a
V-shape in front of them. Call each child's name as you roll the ball
to them and invite them to roll it back to you. When they are rolling
and receiving the ball with confidence, ask each child to roll it to
another child. Use their names: Charlie, please roll the ball to Sara.
When you are sure that the children know each other's names, invite
the children to call out another child's name as they roll the ball in
their direction. Continue until everyone has had a turn at rolling and
receiving the ball.

Questions to ask
Is it just as easy to roll and catch if you are kneeling? Who can keep
their eyes on the ball all the time? Is it easiest rolling or receiving?
Would it be just as easy with a small ball? (Try it.)

For younger children
Keep the circle small so that the children's legs act as a funnel for the
ball when aiming and catching.

For older children
Try the activity standing up. Then progress to throwing and catching
over a short distance.

Follow-up activities
● Throw a balloon in
the air, call out a
name and encourage
that child to catch it.
Now invite the
children to do the
same for each other.
● Play a game of
skittles.
● Roll a large
sponge ball and see if
you can catch the
children as they dart
and dodge.
● Include any
children with visual
impairment by using
a musical ball or a
brightly coloured
shiny cylinder (make
it yourself, filled with
pulses or dry pasta).

COPY CATS

Learning objective
To think up and to
imitate actions.

Group size
Ten to 12 children.

What you need
An open floor space, a cassette recorder and tape of rhythmic music.
An extra helper to work the cassette recorder.

What to do
Gather the children in a circle, standing on the floor. Ask the children
to listen for the music and then copy what you do. Ask for the music
to be started and choose an action to do, such as rubbing your tummy,
for the children to copy. Stop the music and ask the children to think
of their own actions for everyone else to copy. Repeat the music while
the children take turns to be the leader, still standing in their places
within the circle.

Once the children are familiar with the activity, begin to move
around in a circle, again encouraging the children to copy your
movements. Try jumping, running on tiptoes, walking with your hands
on your head, clapping your hands behind your back for example.
Praise the children for copying well, and invite children to lead if
they would like to.

Questions to ask
Close your eyes: can you still copy me? Can you copy two things at
once (rub your tummy and pat your head)? When is it really helpful
to copy each other? Do you ever copy mum or dad as they do things?
Does anyone copy what you do sometimes?

For younger children
Keep the actions simple, and stay sitting down in your circle.

For older children
Think of actions which need more careful co-ordination such as
skipping, hopping, touching the tip of your nose, putting finger and
thumb tips together.

Follow-up activities
● Sing the action
song 'Everybody do
This' from *Okki-tokki-
unga*, (A&C Black).
● Use copying to
teach the children
some simple signs,
particularly if you
have children with
hearing or
communication
difficulties. Ask the
parents of any child
who signs to help
you with ideas for
this.
● During an art and
craft activity invite
the children to copy
your simple colours
and strokes.
● Play 'Follow-my-
leader' all around
your room or
outdoor play area.

PARACHUTES

Learning objective
To develop co-
ordination, co-
operation and control
in a large group.

Group size
Eight children and over.

What you need
At least four adult helpers, parachute: you are unlikely to have access to a real parachute, so compromise with an old king-size sheet, rounding off the corners so that it is shaped like an octagon or a circle. A large enough space to spread the parachute/sheet out. A coloured feather and a sponge ball (at least 15 cm in diameter).

Setting up
Lay the parachute/sheet out flat in the centre of the floor.

What to do
Ask the children to sit cross-legged around the edge of the sheet, and spread them out so that they are evenly spaced around the edge, interspersed by your four helpers at the four points of the compass. Place the coloured feather in the centre of the sheet. Ask the children to pick the sheet up very gently, trying to keep the feather in the centre. Praise the gentle movements and group co-operation that this skill needs. Now show the children how to make the feather jump in the air, show them how to slacken their hold a little, and then all pull the sheet taut on your count of three.

Remove the feather and place the ball in the centre. See whether the children can raise the sheet up without the ball rolling off.

Finally, enjoy some 'parachute' games together. Make 'waves' and 'calm' by shaking and tightening the sheet. Invite all the children to hide underneath whilst the four helpers hold it in a tent. Invite named children to exchange places whilst the sheet is raised then floated gently down on them. Ask the four helpers to make the sheet into a 'rippling sea' while named children 'paddle' across it.

Questions to ask
What happens if we pull at different times? Are there other times when we all have to work together? What does the wavy sheet remind you of? Who knows what a 'parachute' is?

For younger children
Use a smaller sheet and keep the circle fairly small.

For older children
Ask the children to contribute their own ideas for making movements and shapes using the sheet.

Follow-up activities
● Paint parachute pictures for a brightly coloured wall display.
● Provide frames and props for the children to make tents. Provide a selection of sheets so that the children have to learn about choosing the appropriate size for the task.
● Make silver fishes from card and foil to 'float' on your parachute sea.

STEPPING STONES

Learning objective
To develop balancing and co-ordination skills.

Group size
Any size; one helper to five children

What you need
A large space and a non-slip surface. A selection of mats and low apparatus such as a small safety mat, a low gymnastics bench, some rubber-backed carpet samples, and large beanbags.

Setting up
Arrange your assortment of 'stepping stones' in a large circle for the children to sit on.

What to do
Invite the children to take off their shoes and socks and sit on the apparatus while you explain the activity. Challenge the children to draw up their legs so that no part of them is touching the floor or the 'river'. Sing 'Row, Row, Row the Boat' as you rock from side to side, still staying balanced on the 'stepping stones'. Now challenge the children to move all the way around the ring without touching the floor. Pretend that the floor is water and that you are using real stepping stones.

Move around with the children to encourage them, to supervise safety, and to control the speed. Re-arrange the apparatus to make new challenges and new combinations. Finish with a 'Follow-my-leader' game around your circle of apparatus.

Questions to ask
Which stepping stones were the most difficult to balance on? Did you have to move slowly or quickly? Could you do it with your eyes closed? What other ways can you think of to cross a river?

For younger children
Keep the apparatus at ground level and the spaces between shorter.

For older children
Challenge the children by making the balance and control needed all the more challenging by selecting narrower stepping stones and introducing slight gaps and sharper angles between the apparatus.

Follow-up activities
● See if you can all hold hands in your circle of 'stepping stones'.
● Mark out a huge spiral with chalk on paving and invite the children to walk all the way along it without losing their balance.
● Provide a selection of found materials and apparatus and invite the children to construct their own 'stepping stones' circle.

TOE TO TOE

Learning objective
To encourage
movement and co-
ordination of different
parts of the body.

Group size
Ten to 12 children.

What you need
Space for you all to stand in a circle, one pace apart. An extra adult helper.

What to do
Help the children stand in a regular circle by asking them to join hands, then drop hands and stand still. Tell them that you are going to pass different messages around the circle, using different parts of your bodies. Explain that first, your toes are going to meet each other! Ask the child on your left to touch toes with you. Then encourage the child to touch toes with the next child in the ring. Help this action to be passed all around the circle, child by child, with help and encouragement from your helper who can move around the outside of the circle aiding where required.

Now 'pass' shoulder touches, knee touches, elbow touches, fingertip touches and even back touches. Praise the children for doing this gently, and for keeping their balance.

Questions to ask
Ask the children for good ideas for this activity. When do we use our bodies to say 'hello'? (Practise shaking hands around the circle, and waving to each other in turn.)

For younger children
Keep a helper close by to support the child's balance.

For older children
Try touching thumb to thumb, forehead to gentle forehead, heel to heel, elbow to elbow and so on.

Follow-up activities
● Make a circular pattern with everyone's hand print in different coloured paints touching at their sides in a complete circle.
● Start a daily greeting song with a handshake passed all around the circle.
● Send an action around the circle, each to be passed and copied child to child.

MY SPACE

Learning objective
To think about personal spaces and to copy sequences of movement.

Group size
Eight to ten children.

What you need
A large clear floor space and a mat for each child (large enough for two children to sit on). Picture books or illustrations about islands, photocopiable activity sheet on page 63, as a talking point.

Setting up
Spread the mats out evenly in a large circle, with one mat's distance between each.

What to do
Gather the children in a smaller circle in the centre of your mats, sitting on the floor. Tell the children that you are going to play a pretend game about islands. Talk about islands so that the children understand what they are, and show your books, illustrations and the photocopiable page. Explain that each child will have their own island, and can invite friends to swim across and visit them. Close your eyes and imagine what your island will be like.

Now ask each child to find their own 'island' and sit on it. Talk them through the day as they role play waking up, finding food and drink, swimming in the sea, and making their shelter. It is now tea time. Ask one of the children if they would like another to visit them for tea. Go round the circle until everyone is paired up, but allow a child to remain alone if they wish to. Help the children to make the swimming movements and to raise their feet high when paddling in the shallow waves. Repeat one more time so that everyone who wants to has a chance to invite a visitor.

Questions to ask
What would you like your island to be like? Will there be trees? Will there be animals? Close your eyes and imagine. What will you find for tea when your friend comes to visit you? Did you like to be alone on your island or was it good when a friend came too? Can you think of other times when it is good to be on your own, and good to have a friend with you? What do we mean by being 'private'?

For younger children
Provide real props for the role play: a cardboard box to shelter in, shells as plates and cups.

For older children
Extend the role play so that the children imagine more detail and mime more complicated sequences of movement.

Follow-up activities
● Sit at tables and complete the activity sheet on page 63.
● Make a table-top model of an island together out of craft and found materials.
● Make garlands of crêpe paper flowers which the 'visitors' can wear.

CATERPILLARS

Learning objective
To crawl and tunnel within the circle.

Group size
Six children at a time.

What you need
Items for an obstacle course: vinyl play tunnel, cardboard boxes, low bench, cellular blanket, chairs and tables. Smooth floor surface for crawling on. Extra adult helpers.

Setting up
Construct a simple obstacle course in a circle for crawling and tunnelling using whatever materials available provided it is safe and can be supervised easily. For example: a vinyl play tunnel, cardboard boxes open at each end, a low bench to crawl along, a cellular blanket to crawl beneath, a tunnel made of chairs and sheets. Warn parents that you are going to enjoy a crawling and tunnelling game together so that the children can wear suitable PE clothing.

What to do
Gather the children in a smaller circle in the centre of your obstacle course, sitting on the floor. Show them the course and talk about all the ways the children might pretend to be caterpillars and move through it.

Now set the children off one by one, allowing a safe distance between them and share their fun and enjoyment as they find different ways of travelling the course. Have enough helpers standing by to help with the difficult parts or to hold covers straight while children are tunnelling beneath them.

Finish by asking the children to join the circle again to talk about the activity as a group and round off with an appropriate story such as *The Very Hungry Caterpillar* by Eric Carle (Hamish Hamilton) or song such as 'Five Caterpillars Crawling on a Wall' (to the tune of 'Ten Green Bottles').

Questions to ask
Which things will you climb over? Which will you crawl through? Do caterpillars spend all their lives crawling? Can you think of other ways of making tunnels? Have you seen a baby crawling around? Where have you seen a tunnel in your town/countryside?

For younger children
Keep the course simple, using rigid materials such as boxes and shaped tunnels rather than blankets and covers.

For older children
Provide the materials and let the children help you to construct the course, using the children's own ideas as well as your modifications.

Follow-up activities
● Make cardboard tunnels to use with the train set or the car mat.
● Play an imagining game, crawling on hands and knees and thinking about what the world must look like to a baby.
● Use outdoor obstacle courses as a feature for a non-competitive sports day, or use an indoor course as a useful wet-day alternative.

Encourage your children's creative development with these activities involving dance, exploring sounds and smells, composing songs and using their bodies in creative ways.

MAYPOLE DANCE

Learning objective
To decorate a maypole and enjoy a simple dance.

Group size
Six children.

What you need

Play indoors or out. If you are outside you need a strong post (two to three times the height of the children), if you are indoors use a sturdy hat stand or free-standing pole. Stapler and staples, six different coloured ribbons (each one-and-a-half times the length of the pole), coloured tissue paper, a tape of country dance music.

Setting up

Attach the ribbons evenly around the top of the pole, doubling the tops of the ribbon over to form a thick wedge.

What to do

Gather the children together and explain that in the past people used to decorate a maypole in their village and dance around it to celebrate the coming of spring. Show the children how to use the coloured tissue paper to make paper flowers and streamers to decorate the top of the pole. Add these to the pole as the children complete them.

Now teach the children a simple maypole dance. Arrange the six children around the pole each holding one end of a ribbon so that it comes straight out from the top of the pole, but makes a slight curve so that it is not pulled tight. Turn alternate children so that they face in opposite directions, holding the ribbon in their hand which is nearest to the pole. Three will therefore hold it in their right hands and three in their left. Show each child the direction they will walk in. Show the three facing clock-wise how to pass on the inside, and the three going anti-clockwise how to pass on the outside. Slowly walk through the sequence so that the children understand what to do. Remind them to walk and not to overtake each other. When you are confident that the children know what to do, play some suitable country dance music while they perform the finished 'dance'.

Questions to ask

What other times of year do we celebrate? What happens in springtime? Why do you think people were so pleased when spring came? Can you think of ways we could decorate our maypole?

For younger children

Perform the dance with just two children, moving in opposite directions. A helper can hold their hands if needed.

For older children

Increase the number of ribbons and dancers, making sure that you have an even number.

Follow-up activities
● Perform a maypole dance for parents and families.
● Make collages with pieces of ribbon in a criss-cross design.
● Make tartan pictures with wool or ribbon, using different colour combinations and background colours.

HAND SHADOWS

Learning objective
To make shadow
shapes using fingers
and hands.

Group size
Eight to ten children.

What you need
Two extra helpers, a white sheet, a child's chair, a bright lamp or powerful torch, a copy of the photocopiable activity sheet on page 64 for each child. You will need a darkened corner of the room.

Setting up
Place the light or torch in the darkened corner and hang the sheet in front of it, either held by two helpers or strung safely between the furniture and fittings. Leave enough space between the sheet and the light for a child, helped by an adult, to sit. Experiment to find the best sitting position to make a shadow shape against the sheet, so that an audience sitting the other side of it can clearly see.

What to do
Gather the children in a semi-circle facing the sheet. Invite them to watch as you move behind it and make hand-shape shadows projected on to the sheet. Use the photocopiable activity sheet for ideas. Now invite the children to take turns if they would like to, and move behind the sheet with them to help. Make sure you have an extra helper in the audience to help the viewing children talk about the shadow they can see.

Now sit in a complete circle and repeat the hand shapes, inviting the children to copy you. Take it in turns to make a hand shape for the rest of the circle to copy.

Questions to ask
What does the shape remind you of? What is a 'shadow'? Does this shape look funny, scary, floppy, pointy? Can we still see the shadow if we turn the light up bright?

For younger children
Concentrate on making one simple shadow successfully. Show the children how to make a flying bird or a rabbit with ears.

For older children
Invite older children to invent their own shapes, imaginary and 'real'.

Follow-up activities
● Go outside and see whether you can see your own shadows. Does it matter if the sun is shining or not?
● Make up a shadow puppet play together and perform it for the children's families.
● Show how you can make shadow shapes on walls by pointing a light at a dark wall and interposing your hand shapes. Give each child a copy of the activity sheet to take home so that they can practise shapes on their walls.

JOIN THE BAND

Learning objective
To explore sound from three dimensions.

Group size
The whole group; one helper for every six children.

What you need
A selection of musical percussion instruments: drums and beaters, tambourines, shakers (bought or made), triangles and beaters, castanets, jingle bells, guiros, wooden blocks.

Setting up
Place the musical instruments in a box or tray where they can be easily seen and selected.

What to do
Place the box of instruments in the centre of the circle. Invite each child to come and choose an instrument for themselves. If you have more than ten children, you may prefer to invite children by name to come forward to choose, to avoid everyone trying to choose at once. Make sure all your helpers have an instrument too.

Invite the children to watch you and say 'When I point to you, play your instrument'. Move your finger round the circle of children, using facial expresion to encourage the children to join in as you point. Make a halt sign to each child in turn and say 'When I do this, stop playing your instrument', nod encouragement as they stop what they're playing.

Once the children are familiar with your hand signals, use them to bring in different sounds at different times. Sit children with the same instrument together, so that you can use your signals to bring in whole sections of the 'orchestra' at once.

Questions to ask
Close your eyes and listen to the instrument I am playing. Now open your eyes, can you point to the instrument? Which instruments can play loudly? Which are quieter? Tell me about this sound. Which instrument would make a good sound to go with this story/poem?

For younger children
Play an instrument yourself, encouraging the children to play when you play and to stop when you stop.

For older children
Let them take turns in doing the hand signals and 'conducting' the band. Encourage older children to create different sound patterns.

Follow-up activities
● Play a musical cassette tape and use your hand signals to bring in different sections of the orchestra at different times. Praise the children for looking and listening.
● Tell a story and use the hand signals to bring in different sound effects.
● Agree hand signals for 'loud' and 'soft', and use all your signals to start with a single quiet sound, build up to a cacophony, and gradually fade the sound away again.
● Play a simple rhythm (no more than four beats) and encourage the children to copy.

STREAMER PATTERNS

Learning objective
To create patterns in the air with colourful streamers.

Group size
Ten to 16 children.

What you need
Dowelling rod (1cm diameter), sandpaper, penknife, strong glue and gloss paint (for adult use), 1m pieces of ribbon in several different colours, a wide floor space (possibly out of doors on a still day or in a large hall).

Setting up
Make a streamer for each child using the dowelling cut to lengths of 15 cm. Use sandpaper to round off the sharp edges, make a slit in one end and insert the end of a piece of ribbon. Secure with strong glue. You can also paint the handles with gloss paint to contrast with the ribbon colours.

Simplify this activity by asking the children to hold one end of the pieces of ribbon, though the effect is not so spectacular.

What to do
Give each child a streamer and ask them to copy everything you do. At first, they will want to experiment with their streamers, so let them run around the play area holding their streamers high. Encourage them to wave them up and down and watch the waves they make.

Now stand in a circle, evenly spaced and about a metre between each child. Hold your streamer high and invite the children to copy you. Wave it in wide strokes to left and right, high up and low down. Make it slither like a snake. Make it jerk like a firework. Make figure-of-eights in the air. Crouch down and make the same movements close to the ground. Finally, leave your circle formation as you invite the children to 'follow-my-leader' around the space, making shapes and patterns with your streamers as you go.

Questions to ask
What does this shape remind you of? Can you make your streamer wavy like the sea? What sort of pattern would a jumping firework make? What colours shall we put together in our circle?

For younger children
Play this activity indoors and make wavy patterns across the floor.

For older children
Invent dances to do with your streamers and accompany these with sound effects or music.

Follow-up activities
● Make a Chinese dragon together out of painted sheets and a huge mask.
● Make a wall frieze of flying kites, using ribbons and colourful paper.
● Show the children a video of a gymnastics display with streamers and then create your own display and invite parents to watch.

STORMY SEAS

Learning objective
To make up a group sound story.

Group size
12 to 20 children.

What you need
The 'parachute' used on page 46, or a large sheet, a selection of musical percussion instruments, cardboard boxes, card sheets, scissors, glue and sticky tape, paint, foil, safety pins, green and blue crêpe paper.

Setting up
Set up a craft table and a painting area with all the art and craft materials required. Prepare the outlines of a brief story about a boat out on a stormy sea.

What to do
Encourage the children to join you in small groups of four to six to help build a cardboard boat. Make it heavy enough to rest on a waving sheet without falling over, and paint it to look realistic. Help the children to cut streamers of crêpe paper to make seaweed and to cut out card fish shapes and to cover them with foil. Decorate the sheet with the strings of seaweed and fishes, attaching them yourself to one side of the sheet with safety pins.

Gather the children cross-legged in a circle and tell them your story. Invite a few of the children to choose different musical instruments to represent the waves, the storm and the calm afterwards. Ask the other children to hold the sheet around its edge. Retell the story as you make waves on the sheet and accompany it with sound effects. Show your finished sound story to parents.

Questions to ask
What instrument would make a good sound to go with the thunder? What else could we have in our story? What should happen at the end? How can we make our story even more exciting?

For younger children
Involve younger children by giving them the instruments to make the storm.

For older children
Let them help you make up the story and plan the effects.

Follow-up activities
● Mount your boat on a table-top display with shiny waves, seagulls suspended above and the card/ foil fish in the sea.
● Make up a story about a message in a bottle and 'write' appropriate messages.
● Make floating boats to use in the water tray or paddling pool.

BUILD A SONG

Learning objective
To compose a group song.

Group size
Six to eight children.

What you need
It is helpful if you can have a musician for this activity: a guitar player could strum G and D chords to keep the pitch steady or a keyboard player could pick out a simple familiar tune, such as 'Three Blind Mice'.

What to do
Gather the children in a circle, sitting on the floor. Warm up by singing a couple of familiar songs together. Tell them that now they are going to make up their own song. Talk about what it should be about and agree a tune. Now ask the children for ideas and use your ingenuity to fit the ideas to a rhythm or well-known tune. If you are not used to singing, fit their ideas into a rap rhythm instead. Keep the song very simple and short so that you can all remember it, such as this one, sung to the tune of 'Three Blind Mice':

Three sparkly fireworks
Three sparkly fireworks
All went 'Pop!'
All went 'Pop!'
The rocket shot into the sky
And all the children looked up high
And Mrs Thoms said 'My oh my!'
On Bonfire Night.

The finished song is likely to be a mixture of the children's ideas and your rhymes. Do not worry if it does not scan; the important thing is that the children should feel that they 'own' the song.

Questions to ask
What would you like our song to be about? Shall we use a tune that we know or make up a new one? Can you think of a word which rhymes or sounds like 'sky'?

For younger children
Encourage them to adapt a song with which they are already familiar, such as 'This is the way...' to the tune of 'Here We Go Round the Mulberry Bush'.

For older children
Expect older children to contribute ideas about the kinds of words and rhythms you could use.

Follow-up activities
● Involve the children's own ideas when putting together a festival concert or nativity play.
● Provide a keyboard and encourage children to make up their own pieces of music.
● Gather a display of unusual sounds and instruments: wind chimes, rainmakers and gongs for the children to use in their songs and sound creations.

SMELL AND TELL

Learning objective
To guess smells and
fragrances.

Group size
Eight children.

What you need
A selection of identical clear plastic containers with lids, each with a
different fragrance in, include: perfume, vinegar, spice, tomato
ketchup, honey or jam, coffee granules, drinking chocolate. Add other
fragrances with which the children are familiar. Paper to cover the
outside of the jars so that they all look alike, a tray. CARE! Make sure
that the fragrances are safe to smell for all children; be aware of any
allergies or strong dislikes. If the children are handling food, make
sure they wash their hands and do not share the same portion. Give
clear health and safety rules.

Setting up
Prepare and cover the plastic containers. Arrange them on a tray.

What to do
Gather the children in a circle, sitting on the floor. Talk about different
smells. Now remove the covers and introduce your containers, passing
each one round in turn for the contents to be smelled. Allow each
child to hold the container as they smell so that they are in control,
and pass any child by if they are anxious. Talk about the smells and
see whether the children can identify any of them.

Questions to ask
What is your favourite smell? What smells do you hate most? (Take
all suggestions seriously and do not overreact to their comments.)
Which of these smells do you like? Can you tell what this is just by
smelling it? What do we use to smell with? What animals have a
good sense of smell? Why do you think that is?

For younger children
Stay with three very obvious smells: perfume, chocolate, orange juice.

For older children
Pass round some herbs and spices to be smelled and talked about.

Follow-up activities
● Provide a 'smells
table' for the children
to mix and concoct
their own smell
containers.
● Have a guessing
table which children
can visit, matching
cards of food to the
bottle containing
that smell.
● Use and talk about
smells with children
who cannot see:
helpers wearing one
particular perfume,
the home corner with
its own fragrance, a
dash of perfume in
the water tray, a
clean smell from the
wash area, a coffee
smell from the
kitchen door.

FEELING IS BELIEVING

Learning objective
To identify objects by touch.

Group size
Eight to ten children.

What you need
A drawstring bag which can be loosely tied. A selection of objects easily identifiable by their shape (toy train, metal teapot, large spoon, plastic mug, teddy bear, hairbrush, triangle, plastic plate, sponge). Include one or two unusual items.

Setting up
Set up a screen and a table so that you can reach behind and place an object into the bag without the children seeing.

What to do
Gather the children in a circle. Pass round the items you have chosen one by one. Encourage each child to feel each item and encourage them all to talk together about its properties. Talk about any unusual items and introduce their names.

Now explain that you are going to choose one thing and hide it in a bag. You will pass it all the way round the circle for the children to feel, but they must not tell what it is yet. When the object has been passed all around the circle, invite the children all together to say what the item was.

Questions to ask
Is it soft or hard? Is it long or round? Does it have pieces sticking out? Is it hollow? Does it make a noise when you shake it? Try putting gloves on: is it still easy to feel with your hands?

For younger children
Keep the selection of objects familiar and use only four things.

For older children
Invite an older child to choose an object from around the room whilst the other children close their eyes (use a helper to ensure it is appropriate). Ask that child to place the object in the feely bag and pass it round for you all to guess.

Follow-up activities
● Play a blindfold game with a scarf (if the children are happy to). Help the children gently touch each other's hair to guess who it is they have met.
● Arrange a texture table with a range of found and made materials to be touched, felt, talked about and explored.
● Make collages with different textures of materials. Close your eyes to enjoy how it feels.

PHOTOCOPIABLES

Name _____

Tabatha had beautiful whiskers and a long silky tail. She was the prettiest

 that Peter had ever seen.

One day, he left her in the kitchen with some fish and a bowl of  .

He went into the sitting room to watch his favourite programme on the

 . Suddenly he heard a loud crash!   He opened the

into the kitchen and there was Tabatha hiding underneath the

The book shelf had broken and a big story  had fallen into Tabatha's

food and frightened her.

Peter picked her up, sat on a  and stroked her until she felt

better.   Later, Peter helped to fix the shelf with a  and nails.

Name _____

Colour and cut out to
make a number line or
five number cards.

Name _____

Colour and cut to make a roundabout pony.

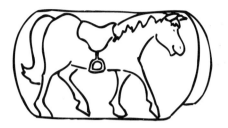

cut out along this line

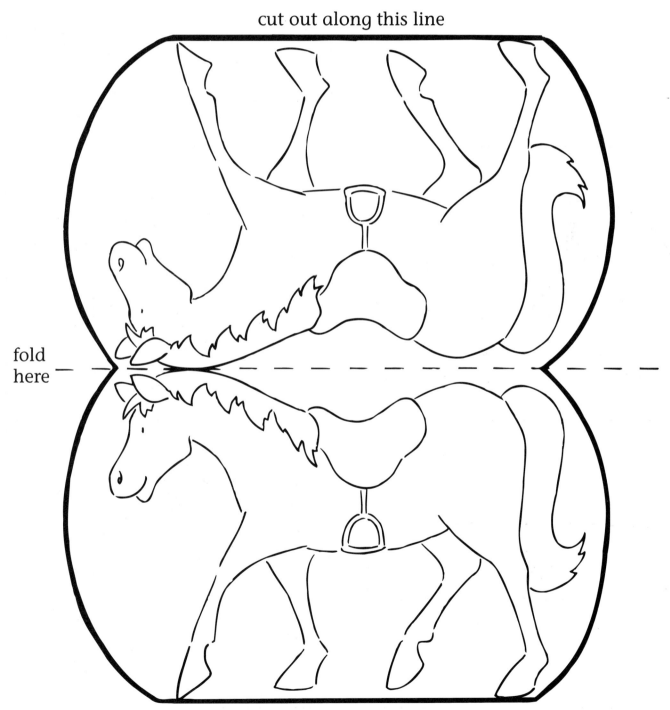

fold
here

Name _____

Name _____

This is your island.
Draw a picture of yourself on your island.
Would you like to draw a friend there too?

Name _____

Practise making these shadows on your wall.

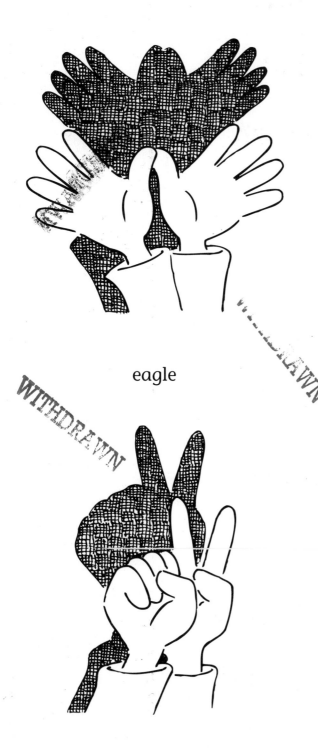

eagle

dinosaur

rabbit

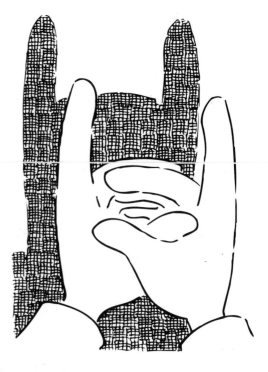

batman